FACTS OF AUSTRALIA

INTERESTING STORIES AND TRIVIA ABOUT THE LAND DOWN UNDER

ELLA WALLABY

Contents

Welcome To The Land Down Under   1

1. Aussies Love Our Golf!   3

2. The Land of All Wild and Wacky Creatures   4

3. Australia, Big Enough to Land in the CBD?   5

4. The Goon Bag   6

5. Australia Spans a Whopping 2,500 Miles (3,860 km)   7

6. Man Vs Bird?   8

7. Pink Seas!   9

8. World's Longest Fence   10

9. Gigantic Aussie Landmarks Galore!   11

10. Sparring Kangaroos Down Under!   12

11. The Great Vegemite Panic!   13

12. Whimsical Wonders of Australia!   14

13. Ancient Aussie Treasures Unearthed!   15

14. The Iconic Sydney Opera House   16

15. The Cane Toad Invasion!   17

16. The "G'Day" Phenomenon!   18

17. Mystical Down Under: The Bunyip!   19

18. Beware of Drop Bears!   20

19. Lifesavers in the Sky: The Flying Doctor!   21

20. Opal Oasis: Coober Pedy's Treasures!   22

21. Icon of the Red Centre: Uluru's Legacy   23

22. The Quirky Charm of Camel Races   24

23. Conquering the "Big Red" Sand Dune   25

24. The Endless Horizon of Nullarbor Plain   26

25. Australia's Eurovision Extravaganza   27

26. Grazing Giants: Cattle Stations   28

27. Aus' Human Development Index   29

28. Embracing Coastal Bliss   30

29. When Does Your Visa Expire?   31

30. A Toast to Aus' Former Prime Minister   32

31. Australia's Law Enforcemet Irony   33

32. Fraser Island: A Natural Marvel   34

33. Wait... How Many Beaches?   35

34. The Iconic and Popular Reef 36

35. It has it's Own Postcode? 37

36. Beached or Bleached Coral? 38

37. Australia's Affection for Beer 39

38. Australian Rules Football? 40

39. Mount Augustus 41

40. From Joey's to Kangaroos 42

41. Kangaroos Continued? 43

42. Snow in One of the Hottest Coutries? 44

43. Australia's Embraces Diversity 45

44. As Mentioned, Aussies Love Their Beer! 46

45. Life on Mars or Just Australia? 47

46. Mad Max: Fury Road (2015) 48

47. Try and Dodge This! 49

48. Why of Course You Can! 50

49. The Devils Marbles! 51

50. The Winged Nation 52

Hey There 53

51. Trams Here, There, Everywhere! 55

52. The Napoleon Pear Tree 56

53. How'd You Buy This Book?   57

54. First Female Prime Minister!   58

55. The Coat Hanger of Australia   59

56. Aussie's Largest Marsupial   60

57. World's Largest Opal   61

58. Camels? What?   62

59. When It Rains, It Pours, Not Here!   63

60. Have You Voted yet?   64

61. World War II   65

62. Golden Deserts to Gold Rushes   66

63. Lamingtons   67

64. Tim Tams   68

65. Pavlova   69

66. Anzac Biscuits   70

67. Iron Ore   71

68. Coal   72

69. Natural Gas   73

70. The Gold Never Stops   74

71. Vineyards for Days   75

72. Lamb and Beef for Everyone   76

73. Crocodile Dundee (1986)   77

74. ANZAC Day in Australia   78

75. Strictly Ballroom (1992)   79

76. Blue Bottles in the Water?   80

77. Three Million Square Mile Rock   81

78. Shark Bait   82

79. Supply and Demand?   83

80. Australia, Known for its Stability   84

81. An Apology From All Australians   85

82. Fair Go for All!   86

83. Highway to Hell!   87

84. Fastest 100m Freestyle   88

85. Grand Slam Tennis   89

86. Aho'y Sailor   90

87. Oldest Sky Diver for a Good Cause   91

88. 1,206 Push-ups in One Hour?   92

89. Safety First!   93

90. The Rubix Cube Master   94

91. Plastic Notes? Yes Please!   95

92. Smokers Beware   96

93. Australia is All About Equality   97

94. Australia's Record-Breaking Cold Spells   98

95. Australia's Record-Breaking Hot Spells   99

96. Leading Gender Equality in Soccer   100

97. Australia's Bioluminescent Beaches   101

98. Numbat or Wombat?   102

99. Australia and Their Lost PM   103

100. Poo in All Shapes and Sizes   104

101. Australia: Too Cool for Volcanic School   105

Trivia   106

Trivia Answers   123

How'd You Score?   127

Thank You   130

Welcome To The Land Down Under

G'day mate!

Welcome to "Facts of Australia - Interesting Stories and Trivia About The Land Down Under," a ripper exploration of Australia's diverse landscapes, unique wildlife, and rich cultural history. This book, written by the one and only Ella Wallaby, is a bonza treasure trove of insights into this extraordinary continent that captures the imagination of travelers and locals alike.

This book celebrates Australia's stunning natural beauty, intriguing history, and vibrant culture. Through my experiences and extensive research, you are invited to discover the fascinating stories, people, and places that make Australia unique. From the buzzing cities to the rugged Outback, from the ancient traditions of Aboriginal Australians to the modern-day lifestyle, every page is chockers (full) with exciting facts and engaging trivia.

In these pages, you will find a collection of 101 fair dinkum (authentic and genuine) facts, each shedding light on the facets of Australian life, geography, history, and society. These facts are complemented by 50 ripper trivia questions designed to test your knowledge and deepen your understanding of Australia. Whether you're a curious traveler, a passionate historian, or someone who loves a good trivia challenge, this book offers something for everyone.

The book's first section presents a comprehensive look at Australia's many wonders, from its geological beauties to its iconic landmarks and cultural achievements. The second section, the trivia, not only provides interesting facts but also invites you to interact test your Aussie knowledge and maybe pick up some more about the vast and varied land of Australia.

So, chuck on your cork hat, grab a cold one, and embark on this bloody bonza journey with "Facts of Australia—Interesting Stories and Trivia About The Land Down Under." Let me, Ella Wallaby, guide you through the captivating tales and secrets of this incredible continent. Get ready to explore the wonders of Australia and test your knowledge of the land Down Under!

1. Aussies Love Our Golf!

Did you know that Australia boasts the world's longest golf course? Spanning an incredible distance of over 850 miles (1,368 km), this mammoth course offers golfers the ultimate challenge across vast and diverse landscapes. From rugged outback terrain to stunning coastal vistas, players can tee off against the backdrop of Australia's breathtaking scenery. So, if you're up for an epic golfing adventure, grab your clubs and get ready to conquer the longest course on the planet Down Under!

2. The Land of All Wild and Wacky Creatures

Australia is known for its wild, creepy crawlies and home to some of the world's deadliest snakes. In fact, out of the top twenty-five most venomous snakes worldwide, twenty-one of them can be found in Australia. These slithery reptiles include the fierce Inland Taipan and the notorious Coastal Taipan, showcasing the incredible biodiversity of Australia's wildlife. If you are ever exploring the wilderness in Australia, it is important to stay alert and respect the unique and dangerous creatures that inhabit this land.

3. Australia, Big Enough to Land in the CBD?

Did you know that Perth boasts a unique distinction among cities worldwide? It's the only city where aircraft can land in its Central Business District (CBD). Thanks to the Perth Airport, conveniently located just ten Miles (17 km) from the city center, planes can soar over the urban skyline and touch down amidst the bustling cityscape. This feature adds to Perth's allure, offering travelers a one-of-a-kind experience as they arrive in the heart of this vibrant Australian metropolis.

4. The Goon Bag

Did you know that Australia has a unique outdoor drinking game called "Goon of Fortune"? This game involves attaching wine casks or "Goon bags" to a rotating clothesline and then spinning it. When the clothesline stops, the person closest to the selected Goon bag has to take a swig from the bag! This fun and creative game is a testament to Australian innovation and their love of communal gatherings. It's an excellent way to enjoy wine while having fun with friends and family. So, the next time you're in Australia, try your hand at the Goon of Fortune game and experience the country's festive and playful spirit.

5. Australia Spans a Whopping 2,500 Miles (3,860 km)

Did you know that Australia is even bigger than you might imagine? It's almost the same size as the mainland USA, measuring 4,662 by 2,897 miles (7,503 by 4,662 km), but with a significantly smaller population! This vast land, Down Under, stretches far and wide, boasting diverse landscapes, from stunning coastlines to rugged outback regions. So next time you picture Australia on the map, remember that it's a colossal continent with plenty of room to roam despite having fewer people than its American counterpart.

6. Man Vs Bird?

Did you know about the Great Emu War of 1932? Australia found itself in an unusual battle against a formidable foe: the emus! The Australian military engaged in a unique conflict with these flightless birds in Western Australia, aiming to control their destructive impact on agricultural lands. Despite their efforts, the emus emerged victorious, showcasing the resilience and adaptability of these iconic Australian birds. It's a quirky history chapter highlighting the unpredictable encounters between humans and wildlife.

7. Pink Seas!

Have you ever heard of Australia's enchanting Pink Lakes? One of the most captivating is Lake Hillier in Western Australia. Its surreal, bubblegum-pink hue isn't a trick of the light - it's nature's masterpiece! This vibrant coloration results from a magical blend of algae and incredibly high salt levels. The sight of this rosy gem nestled amidst the rugged landscape is mesmerizing, offering visitors a glimpse into the extraordinary wonders of the natural world.

8. World's Longest Fence

What are we talking about? None other than the legendary Dingo Fence spanning an astonishing 3,480 miles (5,600 km)! This mammoth structure holds the title for the world's longest fence, a true feat of engineering and ingenuity. Spanning the southeastern region of Australia, what is its main aim? To shield valuable livestock from roaming dingoes. So, when you admire its vastness, it's more than a barrier; it signifies Australia's pioneering ethos and dedication to preserving its ecosystems.

9. Gigantic Aussie Landmarks Galore!

Down under, Australia boasts a peculiar collection of colossal creations known as the "Big Things." From a mammoth banana to an enormous pineapple and even a giant prawn, these oversized sculptures pepper the landscape, capturing the imagination of locals and tourists alike. As quirky landmarks and must-see attractions, they stand as whimsical symbols of Australia's penchant for embracing the extraordinary in everyday life.

10. Sparring Kangaroos Down Under!

In Australia's sprawling landscape, kangaroos aren't merely iconic figures; they're renowned for their impressive boxing abilities. Among these marsupials, the males, referred to as bucks, often partake in spirited bouts, showcasing their strength and agility as they compete for dominance or seek the affection of potential mates. These dynamic displays of athleticism contribute to Australia's diverse wildlife scene's captivating appeal and distinctive character.

11. The Great Vegemite Panic!

Amid the "Vegemite Fiasco Down Under" of 2015, Australia was thrown into chaos by a production tweak that led to a brief scarcity of the beloved spread. Across the nation, Aussies were left in a frenzy, grappling with the prospect of a morning devoid of their cherished Vegemite on toast. This event served as a poignant reminder of Vegemite's deep-seated attachment and cultural importance in Australian households, further cementing its status as a culinary icon Down Under.

12. Whimsical Wonders of Australia!

Australia is renowned for its quirky town and landmark names such as Humpty Doo, Useless Loop, Mount Buggery, Woolloomooloo, and Yorkeys Knob. These unique monikers add a touch of humor to the Australian landscape, reminding us of the country's playful spirit and tendency to embrace the unconventional. Each of these places has an interesting origin story behind its name, adding to the rich folklore and legend of the country. Despite their unusual names, these towns and landmarks are popular tourist destinations, attracting visitors from all over the world. They are charming reminders of Australia's whimsical and adventurous nature.

13. Ancient Aussie Treasures Unearthed!

Nestled within the rugged terrain of Western Australia's Pilbara region lies a remarkable discovery: fossilized stromatolites dating back over 3.5 billion years, making them some of the oldest evidence of life on Earth. These ancient relics offer captivating insights into the microbial world of eons past, enriching our understanding of early life forms and the evolution of our planet. This find cements Australia's status as a cradle of primordial history, contributing to the rich tapestry of scientific knowledge about our planet's ancient origins.

14. The Iconic Sydney Opera House

The Sydney Opera House is an internationally recognized icon of Australia, created by Danish architect Jørn Utzon. Its unique design, featuring white shell-like structures, caused controversy during the fourteen years of construction and led to Utzon's resignation from the project. However, the building's distinctive architecture has become admired and recognized worldwide. The Opera House is renowned for its design and exceptional acoustics, with the interior of the main concert hall featuring specially designed acoustic panels and reflectors. The Opera House hosts over 1,500 performances annually, showcasing a wide range of musical and theatrical genres.

15. The Cane Toad Invasion!

In a well-intentioned yet ultimately disastrous move in the 1930s to combat Queensland's sugarcane beetle infestation, Australia introduced cane toads. However, this decision led to unintended consequences as the toads proliferated rapidly, evolving into a formidable invasive species. Their unchecked expansion wreaked havoc on native wildlife, disrupting ecosystems and forever altering the delicate balance of Australia's biodiversity.

16. The "G'Day" Phenomenon!

The term "G'day" originates from the Australian slang "Good Day" and is commonly used as a greeting in Australia. The term began in the early 1900s as a shortened version of the greeting "Good day to you." Since then, it has become a popular and casual greeting among Australians. The famous Australian greeting "G'day!" is not just a word but a representation of the country's relaxed and friendly nature. Australians are known for their friendly personalities; this greeting is a perfect example. So, if you want to add a touch of fun and engagement to your conversation, try saying, "G'day!"

17. Mystical Down Under: The Bunyip!

Within the vibrant mosaic of Australian folklore, the bunyip stands tall as a mythical creature believed to inhabit the nation's waterways, swamps, and billabongs. Stories of the bunyip are as varied as the vast Australian landscape, portraying it as a formidable and enigmatic entity possessing mystical abilities beyond comprehension. If a bunyip and a dropbear were in a mythical showdown, which creature would emerge victorious? Would the bunyip's mystical powers prevail, or would the dropbear's legendary ferocity reign supreme?

18. Beware of Drop Bears!

In the sun-drenched land down under, amidst the rustling eucalyptus groves, stories of the legendary "drop bear" reverberate through the air. A mischievous creation of Australian folklore crafted to delight and occasionally startle unsuspecting tourists. This whimsical tale describes fictional carnivorous koalas lurking in the treetops, poised to plummet upon unsuspecting passersby with gravity-defying precision. While entirely fictional, the story of the drop bear enriches Australia's diverse wildlife folklore, infusing the country's cultural narrative with a delightful blend of amusement and curiosity. So, the Bunyip or the Dropbear?

19. Lifesavers in the Sky: The Flying Doctor!

In the expansive skies over the rugged Australian outback, the Royal Flying Doctor Service of Australia takes flight, serving as a vital lifeline to the isolated and remote regions of the continent. With aircraft meticulously converted into flying hospitals, these courageous pilots and dedicated medical teams navigate vast distances and challenging terrain to provide essential healthcare services to communities far from urban centers. From delivering emergency medical assistance to conducting routine check-ups, their unwavering commitment ensures that everyone in Australia can access critical healthcare!

20. Opal Oasis: Coober Pedy's Treasures!

Deep in the heart of South Australia, amidst the arid landscape, lies the enchanting town of Coober Pedy, renowned as the world's opal capital. Beneath the sunbaked surface, miners toil tirelessly, unearthing precious opals that sparkle with unparalleled brilliance, fueling a thriving underground community. These remarkable gems contribute to creating unique subterranean dwellings where residents seek refuge from the scorching desert heat. With over 95% of the world's opals originating from its depths, Coober Pedy is a glittering testament to the allure of opulent discovery.

21. Icon of the Red Centre: Uluru's Legacy

Uluru, or Ayers Rock, is a testament to Australia's geological and cultural heritage. Revered by Indigenous Australian tribes, it holds profound spiritual significance. Climbing Uluru once allowed and popular among tourists, was banned in 2019 after years of controversy. Today, Uluru symbolizes cultural resilience and reconciliation, urging visitors to respect sacred Indigenous sites and traditions. Explore its beauty and significance through guided walks, cultural tours, and interpretive displays.

22. The Quirky Charm of Camel Races

In the heart of Australia's Outback, amid the expansive red sands and sprawling plains, camel races offer an unexpected and captivating spectacle. These unconventional events attract participants and spectators from far and wide, injecting excitement and humor into the desert landscape. As camels race across the terrain, their hooves stirring up clouds of sand, the atmosphere buzzes with energy and anticipation. These races demonstrate these creatures' remarkable agility and speed and underscore the character of the Australian wilderness.

23. Conquering the "Big Red" Sand Dune

Nestled amidst the vast expanse of the Simpson Desert lies a towering landmark that beckons adventurers and thrill-seekers from far and wide - the "Big Red" dune. As the tallest dune in this rugged terrain, it offers a thrilling sandboarding experience that is hard to match. For those who dare to brave its towering slopes, this magnificent dune provides an unforgettable encounter with the raw beauty of central Australia, leaving them with memories to cherish for a lifetime.

24. The Endless Horizon of Nullarbor Plain

You know how they say Australia is massive, right? Well, let me tell you about the Nullarbor Plain. This place is like the epitome of Australia's vastness. It covers over 77,220 square miles (200,000 square kms), and it's just this ancient limestone stretch with nothing but flat, treeless land. It's like a blank canvas for adventurers, calling them to come and explore. And let me tell you, when you're out there, the horizon seems to go on forever. It's just nature at its rawest and most breathtaking, spread across this stark landscape.

25. Australia's Eurovision Extravaganza

Despite being far from Europe's shores, Australians have embraced the Eurovision Song Contest with fervent enthusiasm. Each year, the nation comes alive with viewing parties, spirited performances, and unwavering support for Australian contenders, showcasing a deep-seated love for music and international camaraderie. Australian contenders, such as Guy Sebastian and Jessica Mauboy, have received widespread support, with the nation rallying behind them as they take the stage to represent their country on the international platform.

26. Grazing Giants: Cattle Stations

In Australia, they don't do things by halves - their cattle stations are the biggest in the world! These sprawling stations are more significant than Israel and serve as guardians of the country's rural economy and land management practices. Not only do they support thriving cattle industries, but they also protect the rugged beauty and natural heritage of the Outback. It's impressive how Australia's agricultural industry has achieved such greatness.

27. Aus' Human Development Index

Australia has secured the second position on the prestigious Human Development Index, which reflects the country's commitment to societal well-being and progress. The nation has implemented various initiatives to promote longevity, education, and a high standard of living for its citizens. One such initiative is the government's healthcare system, which provides quality medical care to all, consequently leading to increased life expectancy. Additionally, Australia has emphasized education by establishing renowned universities and comprehensive schooling programs that help its citizens excel in various fields.

28. Embracing Coastal Bliss

For most Australians, the dream of living by the coast becomes a cherished reality. Four out of five Australians live within a thirty-one mile (fifty-km) radius of the expansive Australian coastline. This widespread phenomenon is a testament to the irresistible allure of Australia's pristine shores. Still, it is also much more than that. From the iconic Bondi Beach in Sydney to the tranquil beaches of Byron Bay, Australia's coastline is a sight to behold. The crystal-clear waters, sandy beaches, and stunning views attract people from all over the world. But for Australians, the coast is more than just a picturesque backdrop. It is a way of life.

29. When Does Your Visa Expire?

Every week, an estimated seventy adventurous tourists succumb to the magnetic allure of Australia, daringly choosing to overstay their visas. Enthralled by the country's diverse landscapes, vibrant culture, and warm hospitality, these visitors are reluctant to bid farewell to the enchanting land Down Under, captivated by its irresistible charm and allure. As a result, many tourists find themselves irresistibly drawn to the laid-back lifestyle, cultural diversity, and natural splendor that define Australia, leading them to extend their visas to continue their exploration of this remarkable land.

30. A Toast to Aus' Former Prime Minister

Bob Hawke, who served as the Prime Minister of Australia from 1983 to 1991, made history by downing two and a half pints of beer in just eleven seconds. This is an incredible feat. captured the imagination of the Australian public and became a symbol of Hawke's charismatic personality. With his characteristic humor, Hawke playfully attributed his remarkable drinking talent to his political success, further endearing himself to the nation. Beyond his beer-drinking prowess, Hawke's lively personality and genuine connection with the Australian people solidified his status as a beloved figure in the nation's folklore.

31. Australia's Law Enforcemet Irony

The beginning of the Police Force consisted of the most well-behaved convicts. Using former convicts as custodians of law and order reflects Australia's pragmatic approach to governance. It highlights the resourcefulness and adaptability inherent in Australian society. This historical quirk underscores the evolution of Australia's police force and its unique journey from its convict origins to its modern-day role in upholding justice and maintaining social order.

32. Fraser Island: A Natural Marvel

Tucked away in the vast wilderness of Australia, Fraser Island is the world's largest sand island and a symbol of the country's unparalleled natural diversity. This ecological haven boasts breathtaking views, ancient rainforests, and pristine beaches, welcoming adventurers and nature enthusiasts to explore its wonders. It offers a kaleidoscope of ecosystems, ranging from majestic dunes dominating the skyline to serene freshwater lakes in its heart. Visitors can encounter rare wildlife, marvel at the island's distinctive geological features, and immerse themselves in the serenity of its natural beauty.

33. Wait... How Many Beaches?

Did you know that Australia is home to 10,685 beaches? Embarking on a quest to explore each one of them would take approximately twenty-nine years! That's right, this epic journey isn't just a simple trip - it's a true odyssey, an adventure of a lifetime. Imagine the thrill of uncovering the hidden gems that await along its vast and varied coast, from the iconic Bondi Beach to the secluded coves of Tasmania. It's a challenge that beckons intrepid explorers to dive deep into the beauty and mystery of Australia's coastal treasures. So, if you're up for a once-in-a-lifetime adventure, pack your bags, grab your sunscreen, and hit the road to explore the breathtaking beauty of Aus!

34. The Iconic and Popular Reef

Talking about diving, the Great Barrier Reef is the largest living structure on Earth, stretching over 1,400 miles (2,300 km) along the northeastern coast of Australia. It's a majestic testament to the country's marine biodiversity, composed of thousands of individual reefs and islands. The reef teems with vibrant coral formations, mesmerizing marine life, and intricate ecosystems that support an astonishing diversity of species. The reef captures the imagination of scientists, explorers, and adventurers alike. Its size and complexity make it one of the most fascinating ecosystems on the planet, showcasing the beauty and resilience of Australia's environment.

35. It has it's Own Postcode?

The Great Barrier Reef is a UNESCO World Heritage Site and a globally significant natural wonder. It offers a unique postal service within the boundaries of its marine park. This service allows visitors to send postcards that showcase the iconic image of the Great Barrier Reef. It's a beautiful way for visitors to keep a tangible memory of their journey through this natural wonder. Moreover, by sending postcards, visitors contribute to the ongoing legacy of the Great Barrier Reef. They help spread awareness and appreciation for the reef's unparalleled beauty and ecological importance.

36. Beached or Bleached Coral?

Climate change has a profound impact on the Great Barrier Reef. The rising ocean temperatures cause widespread coral bleaching, which threatens the reef's biodiversity. This event underscores the urgent need to address climate change and take immediate action to reduce greenhouse gas emissions. Scientists predict that without action, the reef could lose up to 90% of its coral by 2050. This loss would be devastating for marine biodiversity and the communities that rely on the reef. It is imperative for governments, businesses, and individuals worldwide to collaborate in reducing emissions and transitioning to a low-carbon economy.

37. Australia's Affection for Beer

We've all heard the Aussies like drinking, but do you know how much? It's a part of the cultural fabric, and Australians collectively consume a staggering 449.1 million gallons (1.7 billion liters) of beer yearly. Whether during barbecues, sporting events, or casual gatherings with friends, beer is integral to social gatherings in Australia. This love for beer reflects the lifestyle of Australians. It contributes to the vibrancy of the country's social scene, fostering bonds and shared experiences among communities nationwide. With beer choices from crisp lagers to hoppy ales, beer mirrors Australian society's diverse and eclectic nature, making it integral to the nation's identity and cultural heritage.

38. Australian Rules Football?

Did you know that Australian Rules Football (AFL) was initially created in the mid-19th century to keep cricketers fit during the offseason? However, it soon evolved into a distinct sport with its rules and strategies. Today, AFL is the most popular spectator sport in Australia, with its fast-paced, high-scoring nature, coupled with the physicality and athleticism of its players, capturing the hearts of millions of Australians. The sport's roots in Australian history and its thrilling gameplay have fostered a deep connection between fans and the sport, making it an integral part of the nation's identity and cultural fabric.

39. Mount Augustus

Australia is home to some of the most breathtaking natural wonders on the planet, and Mount Augustus is no exception. Unlike its more famous counterpart, Uluru, Mount Augustus is the world's most significant rock formation, boasting an impressive size and a rich history that dates back millions of years. Its rugged, ancient beauty is genuinely awe-inspiring, inviting adventurers to explore its majestic heights and uncover the stories etched into its ancient stone. Whether you're a seasoned hiker or just looking for a unique and unforgettable experience, visiting Mount Augustus will leave you with memories that will last a lifetime.

40. From Joey's to Kangaroos

Australia's most recognizable animal is undoubtedly the Kangaroo. But did you know there are more than sixty different species of kangaroos in Australia? From the giant and energetic red kangaroos to the small and cute wallabies, there is a lot of variation in size, behavior, and habitat. This diversity of kangaroo species showcases the incredible wildlife that can be found. Whether exploring the lush rainforests and spotting agile tree kangaroos or marveling at the speedy antilopine kangaroos in the Outback, there is always something new and exciting to discover about these fascinating creatures in Australia's diverse habitats.

41. Kangaroos Continued?

Australian cuisine is known for its unique and quirky traits. One such trait is the availability of kangaroo meat in supermarkets. This meat is highly valued for its low-fat content of only one to two percent and its high protein and essential nutrient content such as zinc and iron. Kangaroo meat is healthy and offers a distinct flavor that sets it apart from traditional meats like beef or lamb. Some describe its taste as gamey, while others claim it has a slight sweetness. Either way, it's a unique experience for your taste buds that should not be missed. So, if you ever find yourself in Australia, why not try kangaroo meat?

42. Snow in One of the Hottest Coutries?

Did you know that the Australian Alps are home to some of the most breathtaking views and receive more snowfall each year than Switzerland? Suppose you're a winter sports enthusiast seeking a unique, unforgettable snow-filled adventure. In that case, the Aussie Alps should be on your radar. There's something for everyone, from skiing and snowboarding to snowshoeing and tobogganing. And when you're not out hitting the slopes, you can relax in cozy lodges and enjoy the warm hospitality of the locals. So why not consider swapping your usual snowy destination for a trip to the Australian Alps?

43. Australia's Embraces Diversity

Australia is culturally diverse, with 33% of its population comprising individuals born in another country. This diversity creates a beautiful tapestry of traditions and perspectives, adding vibrancy and depth to Australian society. From the busy streets of Sydney to the remote outback communities, you'll find many languages, cuisines, and customs that make Australia a melting pot of cultures. Australians celebrate and honor the traditions of their neighbors, creating a dynamic and inclusive society that thrives on diversity. Whether it's Lunar New Year, Diwali, or Eid al-Fitr, Australians embrace diversity and cherish the rich tapestry of cultures that make their country unique.

44. As Mentioned, Aussies Love Their Beer!

Did you know that one of Australia's most beloved spreads, Vegemite, has a fascinating origin story? It all started with leftover yeast from beer production. In 1922, a food technologist named Cyril Callister created a spread using the surplus yeast from Carlton & United Breweries in Melbourne. After experimentation and testing, Vegemite was born. Vegemite is unique because of its savory, umami flavor, thanks to its yeast extract base. It's a taste that might take some getting used to for first-timers. Still, for many Australians, it's a beloved childhood memory and a symbol of national pride.

45. Life on Mars or Just Australia?

Just an hour's drive north of Perth in Western Australia, you will discover the mysterious Nambung Desert, home to the enigmatic Pinnacles. Imagine eerie limestone rock formations scattered across the desert landscape, resembling something straight out of "Life on Mars." Their otherworldly appearance sparks the imagination and invites comparisons to extraterrestrial landscapes. But don't worry, brave adventurer, a visit to the Pinnacles is not just a journey to another planet; it's an opportunity to explore the surreal beauty and geological wonders of Western Australia's diverse terrain.

46. Mad Max: Fury Road (2015)

Did you know that the high-octane movie Mad Max: Fury Road (2015), directed by the innovative George Miller, was primarily shot in Namibia's stark Australian outback and barren landscapes? This cinematic epic takes audiences on an intense journey through a dystopian world, where the rugged Australian scenery plays a crucial role in setting the film's apocalyptic tone. The authentic Australian backdrops contribute significantly to the movie's gritty and desolate feel, making it a visual spectacle. Watch for the film's distinctive Australian desert scenes, crucial to its powerful and immersive atmosphere.

47. Try and Dodge This!

Did you know that the 1999 science-fiction film The Matrix used various locations in Sydney to create the futuristic cityscape of "Mega City" in the movie? It's incredible to think that such a groundbreaking and iconic film was filmed, at least in part, in such a beautiful and historic city. As you watch and navigate through the digital realm, keep an eye out for the familiar landmarks of Sydney seamlessly woven into the fabric of this movie. For example, Martin Place, a bustling pedestrian thoroughfare and a popular meeting place for locals, was a pivotal location to bring this dystopian world to life.

48. Why of Course You Can!

Step back in time and experience the glamour of the 1920s with Baz Luhrmann's stunning adaptation of F. Scott Fitzgerald's classic novel, The Great Gatsby (2013). This visually captivating film takes you on a journey through the lavish world of Jay Gatsby and his extravagant parties, filmed in various locations across New South Wales. From the bustling streets of Sydney to the stunning beauty of the Blue Mountains, Luhrmann perfectly captures the essence of the era, transporting you to a time of extravagance and indulgence. So, put on your flapper dress and top hat and get ready for a cinematic adventure like no other, where every scene is a spectacle of Gatsby himself!

49. The Devils Marbles!

Did you know about the fantastic geological marvels called Devil's Marbles? These rocks are also known as Karlu Karlu to the Aboriginal traditional owners. They are not just ordinary boulders but nature's version of the popular Jenga game! These rocks stand tall at up to twenty feet (six meters) and have been balancing themselves for millions of years in a unique rounded and stacked formation shaped by the forces of erosion. If you are in the Northern Territory, be sure to visit these natural sculptures and maybe even try your hand at rock stacking. But be careful not to spoil nature's masterpieces by toppling them over!

50. The Winged Nation

Australia is a birdwatcher's paradise with diverse birds, including the famous laughing kookaburra, majestic emu, and cheeky cockatoo. You can also witness the rainbow of lorikeets and rosellas lighting up the sky with dazzling colors. Don't forget the little penguins waddling along the shores in their adorable tuxedos. With habitats ranging from lush rainforests to vast deserts, Australia is a perfect place to explore the unique and fascinating world of birds. Grab your binoculars, spread your wings, and soar into the land Down Under.

Hey There

I hope you are enjoying the book so far. I just wanted to take a moment to express my sincere gratitude for joining me on this fascinating journey into the heart of Australia's captivating facts. It's been an incredible odyssey filled with discovery, creativity, and lots of tea!

As you might already know, each fact in this collection has been carefully curated to provide you with an insightful glimpse into Australia's unique essence and a spark of wonder. But I would love to hear your thoughts and feedback as well! Your insights, be they expressions of amazement, thoughtful critiques, or your own anecdotes related to this remarkable continent, are truly invaluable to me.

Sharing your experiences and leaving your feedback helps celebrate and disseminate the fascinating aspects of Australian lore and fuels and shapes the direction of my future endeavors.

Your review means a lot. You can leave your feedback on Amazon by scanning the QR code.

Thank you so much for being an integral part of this expedition. Your perspectives enhance this collection and weave us together in the shared joy of uncovering Australia's secrets. Here's to many more discoveries and moments of awe as we delve deeper into Australia's wonders together!

51. Trams Here, There, Everywhere!

Melbourne is famous for having the largest tram network globally, stretching over 150 miles (250 km) and servicing over 200 million passengers annually. But beneath the city's bustling streets lies a hidden marvel: an old tram tunnel shrouded in mystery. Dating back to the early 20th century, this underground passage was a forgotten piece of Melbourne's transit history until its rediscovery in recent times. Initially used for tram operations, the tunnel's exact purpose and history remain partly enigmatic, sparking curiosity among historians and urban explorers.

52. The Napoleon Pear Tree

The Napoleon pear tree in Tasmania, Australia, is not just any ordinary tree. It's one of the oldest and largest pear trees in the Southern Hemisphere and has stood tall since the early 19th century. This tree is significant for its age and size. It is a living link to Tasmania's colonial history and heritage fruit cultivation. Named after the 'Napoleon' variety of pear, popular during the 1800s for its excellent eating and cooking qualities, this tree is a must-see for anyone who loves pears or is interested in Tasmania's agricultural and botanical history. So, if you are on a trip to Woolmers Estate near Longford, why not take a bite out of history?

53. How'd You Buy This Book?

Sydney, Australia has a significant contribution to the development of Wi-Fi technology. Dr. John O'Sullivan and his team of Australian scientists pioneered a revolutionary method for transmitting data wirelessly in the 1990s, which has transformed the way we use the Internet today. Their tireless efforts and innovative ideas laid the foundation for the Wi-Fi technology that we now use seamlessly. It is essential to acknowledge and recognize their innovation, which came out of Sydney and has gifted us with endless possibilities and connectivity.

54. First Female Prime Minister!

Julia Gillard was Australia's first female Prime Minister in 2010 and in the country's history. Serving until 2013, Gillard was a trailblazer for women in politics and achieved many significant milestones during her tenure. She introduced a carbon pricing scheme to tackle climate change, oversaw major education reforms such as the National Curriculum and the Gonski funding model, and established the Royal Commission into Institutional Responses to Child Sexual Abuse. Gillard also played a crucial role in improving Australia's relationship with its Asian neighbors; her legacy as Australia's first female Prime Minister inspires women across the country to pursue leadership roles in politics.

55. The Coat Hanger of Australia

The Sydney Harbour Bridge is an Australian landmark completed in 1932 after eight years of construction. The "Coathanger" was built to connect Sydney's central business district with the North Shore. The bridge spans 3,770 feet (1,149 meters) in length and weighs over 52,800 tonnes, making it one of the largest steel arch bridges in the world. The bridge was constructed with over six million hand-driven rivets and required the labor of approximately 1,400 workers. It also has a set of towers at each end, which are purely decorative and serve no structural function. The bridge offers adventurous visitors the opportunity to climb to its summit for breathtaking city and harbor views.

56. Aussie's Largest Marsupial

During the Pleistocene era, the Australian continent was inhabited by the "giant wombat." This colossal creature stood 5 feet (1.5 m) tall at the shoulder and weighed up to to 6,613 pounds (3,000 kg), dominating the landscape, seen by extensive fossil records across Australia. These fossils highlighted this animal thrived in lush forests and arid regions and suggested an herbivorous diet and possibly social behaviors like group living. The Diprotodon's existence dates back to approximately 25,000 years ago, coinciding with significant climatic changes and the arrival of humans, factors believed to have contributed to its extinction.

57. World's Largest Opal

The Olympic Australis is a precious gemstone discovered in Coober Pedy, South Australia, 1956. It is considered a national treasure owing to its rarity and stunning beauty. Weighing over 17,000 carats, it is the world's most significant and most valuable opal. Although it is priceless, experts have estimated its value to be millions of dollars. The gemstone is renowned for its captivating play of colors that change and shift when it catches the light. The opal displays a range of vibrant hues, such as blues, greens, and reds, which testify to the unique geology of the area where it was found.

58. Camels? What?

Australia is a country known for its unique wildlife, and one animal that has significantly contributed to Australia's biodiversity is the camel. Did you know that Australia has the world's largest population of wild camels? Over 1.2 million camels are estimated to live in the arid regions of central and western Australia today. Camels were first introduced to Australia in the 19th century as a means of transportation and to assist with developing the country's vast interior regions. However, the camels were no longer needed with new transportation technology, and many were released into the wild.

59. When It Rains, It Pours, Not Here!

Australia is a country of great contrasts, and one of the most notable is the vast Outback that covers most of its land area. This arid and semi-arid region is characterized by sparse vegetation, rugged terrain, and extreme temperatures, with some areas receiving less than ten inches (twenty-five cm) of rainfall annually. It is home to various unique flora and fauna, including iconic species such as kangaroos and wallabies, as well as a wide range of reptiles and birds. Today, it's a popular destination for adventurers who seek to explore its vast expanses and discover its hidden treasures.

60. Have You Voted yet?

In Australia, voting in federal and state elections is compulsory for eligible citizens, legally obliging them to cast their vote. Failing to do so may result in a penalty. The rationale behind this practice is to ensure individuals exercise their right to vote, promoting high voter turnout, political engagement, and civic responsibility. Citizens can vote early, by mail, and overseas, with educational resources provided by the government. This has achieved high voter turnout and political engagement since the early 20th century.

61. World War II

Australia played a significant strategic role during World War II due to its vast landscapes. One of the lesser-known incidents in Australia's wartime history is the Battle of Brisbane that took place in 1942. This conflict arose between Australian and American troops stationed in Brisbane, Queensland, and was caused by cultural differences and rivalries between the two allied forces. The Battle of Brisbane was a unique and complex event that highlighted the challenges of maintaining harmony among allied nations during wartime. It stands as a testament to Australia's vital role during World War II and the intricacies of international cooperation during times of conflict.

62. Golden Deserts to Gold Rushes

During the mid-19th century, Australia experienced a significant surge in economic growth, urbanization, and infrastructure development thanks to the discovery of gold. The discovery sparked several gold rushes in the region, attracting droves of immigrants worldwide. This influx of prospectors, eager to strike it rich, played a crucial role in Australia's transformation from a colonial outpost to a thriving nation. The gold rushes, especially those in Victoria and New South Wales, represent a significant chapter in Australia's history and fascinate historians and visitors alike.

63. Lamingtons

Lamingtons are a popular dessert in Australia. They consist of square-shaped sponge cakes dipped in chocolate icing and rolled in desiccated coconut. The origin of the lamington is attributed to a cook at Government House in Queensland who accidentally dropped a piece of sponge cake into chocolate sauce and coated it in coconut to prevent waste. Today, lamingtons are a beloved treat in Australia. They are commonly served at morning teas, fundraisers, and national celebrations such as Australia.

64. Tim Tams

Tim Tams are one of Australia's most beloved treats. These delectable chocolate-coated biscuits filled with rich chocolate ganache were first introduced by the esteemed Arnott's biscuit company in 1964 and have since become an iconic part of Australian culture. With a tempting range of flavors, including original, caramel, and double-coated, Tim Tams has captured the hearts of Aussies nationwide. The "Tim Tam Slam" has become a popular pastime, where Tim Tams are used as makeshift straws for sipping hot beverages. This phenomenon has inspired various creative recipes and variations, cementing Tim Tams' place as an enduring part of Australian culinary history.

65. Pavlova

Pavlova, a popular dessert made from meringue, whipped cream, and fresh fruit toppings, has become a beloved staple at special occasions and celebrations around the world. Though its exact origins are a topic of dispute between Australia and New Zealand, this sweet treat is widely recognized to have been named after the renowned Russian ballerina Anna Pavlova. Many Australians consider the pavlova to be a national dish, and it is commonly served during the holiday season.

66. Anzac Biscuits

Anzac biscuits are a popular sweet treat in Australia and New Zealand, especially on Anzac Day, a national day of remembrance for those who served and died in wars, conflicts, and peacekeeping operations. These crunchy biscuits are made from a mixture of rolled oats, flour, desiccated coconut, sugar, butter, golden syrup, bicarbonate of soda, and boiling water, and have a historical connection to the Australian and New Zealand Army Corps (ANZAC) soldiers during World War I. At that time, the soldiers' loved ones would send them Anzac biscuits as a durable and tasty treat that could withstand the long journey by sea.

67. Iron Ore

Australia's economy heavily relies on the export of iron ore, which contributes significantly to the country's Gross Domestic Product (GDP) and generates employment opportunities for thousands of Australians. The industry is one of the most important export commodities, generating billions of dollars in revenue annually. In 2019, Australia achieved a record high of 833 million metric tons in iron ore exports, with China, Japan, and South Korea as the top three trading partners. Australia's modern infrastructure, large-scale mining operations, and proximity to these major Asian markets have enabled it to maintain a dominant position in the global iron ore market.

68. Coal

Australia's coal industry has been a major contributor to the country's economy. The nation is home to abundant coal reserves that not only support the domestic energy needs but also play a significant role in the global energy market. The industry has been instrumental in generating export revenues and providing a reliable source of power both locally and internationally. Despite increasing concerns over climate change, the coal sector continues to invest heavily in exploring new technologies to lower its environmental impact. With a focus on innovation and sustainability, the industry is poised to contribute to the global energy transition in the years to come.

69. Natural Gas

Australia's substantial offshore natural gas reserves, found in Western Australia and the Northern Territory, position it as a significant player in the global liquefied natural gas (LNG) export market. With a focus on diversifying its customer base, Australia's LNG exports reach a wide range of destinations across the Asia-Pacific region, including key markets such as Japan, China, and South Korea. The country's ability to extract and export natural gas has boosted its economy and helped meet the growing demand for natural gas worldwide.

70. The Gold Never Stops

Australia is a leading global producer of gold, with extensive reserves of this precious metal found in various regions across the country. However, most gold reserves are concentrated in Western Australia, home to some of the world's largest gold mines. The export of gold significantly contributes to Australia's economy. Gold has played a crucial role in shaping Australia's history, with the discovery of gold in the 19th century leading to a gold rush that transformed the country's economy and society. Today, Australia is recognized as one of the world's top gold producers, with the metal being widely used in jewelry, electronics, and other industries.

71. Vineyards for Days

Australia's stunning and diverse landscape hosts some of the world's most extensive vineyard regions. The country's wine production is characterized by its exceptional quality, with renowned varieties such as Shiraz, Chardonnay, and Cabernet Sauvignon crafted into high-quality Australian wines. These wines are cherished and sought-after in Australia and in international markets, including the United States, China, and the United Kingdom. Australian wines have gained a reputation for being some of the best in the world, thanks to the country's unique climate, soil, and winemaking techniques.

72. Lamb and Beef for Everyone

Australia is a leading beef and lamb exporter, with its livestock industry as a vital component of the country's agricultural sector. Aus' climate and vast, open spaces provide ideal conditions for raising high-quality cattle and sheep. Australian beef and lamb products are renowned for their taste and tenderness. Thanks to these attributes, Australian beef and lamb are in demand across global markets, and the country's livestock sector represents a significant contributor to Australia's economy. Asian, North American, and Middle Eastern consumers are the top export destinations for these products.

73. Crocodile Dundee (1986)

Did you know that the famous line "That's not a knife. This is a knife!" was ad-libbed by Paul Hogan during filming? The improvised moment became one of the film's most iconic scenes, showcasing Dundee's Aussie charm in the heart of New York City. The genuine crocodile used in the movie was so well-trained that it reportedly stole the show during filming, leaving the cast and crew in stitches!

74. ANZAC Day in Australia

In Australia, April 25th is a public holiday to honor Australian and New Zealand Army Corps (ANZAC) soldiers who fought at Gallipoli during World War I. People pay their respects to these heroes through dawn services, marches, and wreath-laying ceremonies. Aussies also celebrate the ANZACS by playing two-up, a form of gambling that ANZAC soldiers played during wartime. Playing two-up becomes a legal and widespread activity in pubs and clubs across Australia on ANZAC Day as an exception to its usual prohibition. This tradition is a way for Australians to connect with their history and honor the ANZAC spirit.

75. Strictly Ballroom (1992)

Love in the Ballroom

Baz Luhrmann's 1992 film Strictly Ballroom is a classic Australian movie that has become a cultural icon. The movie was shot on location in Sydney, and its colorful portrayal of Australia's ballroom dancing scene during the 1980s and early 1990s has helped to establish it as an essential cultural artifact. The iconic Love Is in the Air dance scene, widely considered the movie's highlight, took over three weeks to rehearse and film, but its end result was pure magic on screen! Today, Strictly Ballroom is widely regarded as a landmark Australian film, and its popularity has helped to cement Luhrmann's place as one of the country's most celebrated filmmakers.

76. Blue Bottles in the Water?

Australia is renowned for its beautiful coastal waters, home to numerous stunning beaches that attract millions of visitors annually. However, these waters are also home to a potentially dangerous creature - the bluebottle jellyfish, also known as the Portuguese man of war. These vibrant blue creatures, with their striking appearance and venomous tentacles, can be commonly found along Australia's eastern and western coastlines, particularly during the warmer months. Despite their beauty, encounters with bluebottle jellyfish can be painful and even life-threatening. If you see a blue bottle in the water, I'd dip out rather than in!

77. Three Million Square Mile Rock

Australia, the world's sixth-largest country, spans approximately three million square miles (7.7 million square kms). With a population of about 26.69 million people as of 2023, mainly concentrated in coastal urban areas, it has a low population density of 1.34 people per square mile or three people per square kms. In stark contrast, the United States, which has a comparable land area, boasts a much larger population of around 335,893,238, resulting in a population density of approximately 88.46 people per square mile. This comparison highlights Australia's vast, open landscapes against the more densely populated regions of the U.S.

78. Shark Bait

Australia is undoubtedly one of the most fascinating countries in terms of marine life. With over 180 shark species dwelling in its waters, including the great white, tiger, and bull sharks, it's no surprise that Australia is considered a hotspot for shark enthusiasts and researchers alike. Despite their fearsome reputation, shark attacks in Australia are relatively rare, with an average of fifteen incidents reported annually. However, it's worth noting that Australia has one of the highest rates of fatal shark attacks worldwide, accounting for one-third of all shark-related fatalities. It's crucial to understand how we can keep ourself and all the sharks safe

79. Supply and Demand?

Australia exports most of its resources, but it imports goods, including electronics, machinery, clothing, and food products. One significant aspect of Australia's dependence on imports is its reliance on foreign oil and petroleum products to meet its energy needs. Despite having vast reserves of natural gas and coal, Australia imports over 90% of its crude oil and refined petroleum products, making it vulnerable to fluctuations in global oil prices and geopolitical tensions. This heavy reliance on imports highlights the need for sustainable solutions to ensure the country's long-term economic growth and prosperity.

80. Australia, Known for its Stability

Australia's housing market has been a topic of discussion due to soaring prices. The foreign investment has played a significant role in soaring prices. In my area in Sydney, the estimated Sydney's median house price higher at $1.6 million. This influx of foreign investment has led to concerns about housing affordability for local residents, with some arguing that it has contributed to the housing market becoming out of reach for many Australians. To address these concerns and promote affordability and accessibility, the Australian government has introduced policies regulating foreign investment.

81. An Apology From All Australians

On February 13, 2008, Prime Minister Kevin Rudd gave a heartfelt apology to the Stolen Generations on behalf of the Australian government. This significant event marked the official recognition and apology for the injustices suffered by Indigenous Australian children who were taken away from their families by government authorities and church missions from the late 1800s until the 1970s. The apology was a sincere expression of regret, acknowledging the pain, suffering, and trauma experienced by Indigenous communities. It was a crucial step toward reconciliation, expressing our commitment to healing the wounds of the past.

82. Fair Go for All!

Australia is renowned for its "fair go" principle, which is deeply ingrained in the country's culture and values. This principle is based on the belief that everyone deserves an equal opportunity to succeed and live a fulfilling life, regardless of their background or circumstances. It is reflected in Australia's laws, policies, and institutions, which prioritize equality, tolerance, and social justice. The "fair go" principle is not just a vague notion but a fundamental part of Australian identity, guiding everything from education and healthcare to employment and government services. It is a testament to the country's commitment to building a fairer and more inclusive society.

83. Highway to Hell!

Australia is a land of breathtaking beauty, and its vastness is best experienced through the world's longest national highway, Highway 1, also known as the National Highway. Spanning an incredible 9,000 miles (14,500 km), this iconic road circumnavigates the entire continent, connecting major cities, regional centers, and remote outback areas. The highway offers travelers an unparalleled journey through Australia's diverse landscapes, from the lush coastal regions to the stark desert plains, showcasing the country's natural beauty. Driving along this highway is an experience like no other, with stunning vistas, unique wildlife, and rich cultural experiences waiting at every turn.

84. Fastest 100m Freestyle

Cate Campbell, an Australian swimmer, set the world record for the women's 110-yard (100m) freestyle with a time of 52.06 seconds in July 2019. This feat was accomplished at the FINA World Championships in Gwangju, South Korea. Cate Campbell's remarkable achievement was a testament to her own skill and dedication and a reflection of the high standards and level of excellence that Australian athletes consistently strive for.

85. Grand Slam Tennis

Margaret Court, an Australian tennis player, is regarded as one of the greatest athletes in tennis history. She holds the record for the most Grand Slam singles titles won by any player, male or female, with twenty-four titles. Her incredible sports achievements have earned her numerous accolades, including induction into the International Tennis Hall of Fame. Court's success has helped cement Australia's reputation as a powerhouse in the world of tennis, and her legacy continues to inspire young tennis players worldwide. Despite controversy surrounding her personal beliefs, her impact on tennis cannot be denied, and she remains an important figure in Australian sports history.

86. Aho'y Sailor

Australia boasts a rich maritime legacy, highlighted by the incredible achievements of Jessica Watson. In May 2010, at only sixteen, Jessica completed a solo non-stop circumnavigation of the globe by yacht in 210 days, traveling over 23,000 nautical miles (42,596 kms). Her journey made her the youngest person to achieve such a feat, cementing her place in Australian history. Jessica's skill and determination marked a record despite facing numerous challenges, including treacherous weather. They will continue to inspire young sailors globally.

87. Oldest Sky Diver for a Good Cause

Irene O'Shea, a grandmother, made headlines across the world when she set a world record for the oldest skydiver at the age of 102 years old. In December 2018, O'Shea completed a tandem skydive from 14,000 feet (4,267 meters) in the air, becoming an inspiration for people of all ages. The adventurous grandmother's skydiving feat was significant because she did it to raise awareness and funds for the Motor Neurone Disease Association of South Australia. Irene's determination and courage remind us that age is just a number and that it's never too late to pursue our passions and make a difference in the world.

88. 1,206 Push-ups in One Hour?

Eva Clarke, an Australian fitness enthusiast, has made history by setting the world record for the most push-ups in one hour by a female. In November 2019, Eva achieved an incredible feat by completing 1,206 push-ups within sixty minutes, beating the previous record by a margin of seventy-one push-ups. Eva's remarkable achievement has earned her a place in the record books and inspired countless fitness enthusiasts worldwide to push the limits of their physical abilities. Her dedication toward fitness and her unwavering spirit serve as a testament to the indomitable spirit of Australians and their never-give-up attitude.

89. Safety First!

Australia is known for its beautiful landscapes, diverse wildlife, and rich history. However, did you know that Australia was also the first country in the world to implement mandatory seat belt laws? The legislation was introduced in Victoria in 1970, requiring all vehicle occupants to wear seat belts while traveling. This groundbreaking law significantly impacted road safety and has saved countless lives over the years. Today, seat belt laws are in place in countries worldwide. Still, it was Australia that set the precedent for this life-saving legislation. This is one of many ways Australia has been a leader in promoting safety and protecting its citizens.

90. The Rubix Cube Master

Australia has always been known for its incredible achievements, and one such feat that deserves recognition is the fastest time to solve a Rubik's Cube blindfolded. This impressive record was set by Feliks Zemdegs, an Australian speedcuber, in November 2019. Zemdegs stunned the world with his incredible ability to solve the complex puzzle in just 16.22 seconds, all while blindfolded. His feat is a testament to the exceptional talent and dedication of Australian athletes and competitors across all fields of expertise. This record-breaking achievement has certainly put Australia on the map as a nation of innovators and achievers.

91. Plastic Notes? Yes Please!

Australia was the first country to introduce polymer banknotes into circulation. This move by the Reserve Bank of Australia in 1988 replaced traditional paper-based currency with more durable and secure polymer-based notes. This made Australian banknotes more resistant to wear and tear, dirt, and moisture, significantly increasing their lifespan. The use of polymer notes has become a global standard, with many countries worldwide adopting them as well. Australia's pioneering spirit and innovation in introducing polymer banknotes demonstrate its reputation as a nation of trailblazers and innovators, always leading the way in new and exciting developments.

92. Smokers Beware

Known for its progressive policies on public health, one of the most notable examples is the country's role in the global movement to restrict smoking in public spaces. In 1973, Victoria became the first jurisdiction in the world to ban smoking in certain public places, such as theaters, cinemas, and public transport. This groundbreaking legislation marked a significant step in public health and safety, quickly inspiring other regions and countries to follow suit. Today, smoking bans in public spaces are common across the world, and they are widely recognized as an effective way to reduce the harmful effects of secondhand smoke on non-smokers.

93. Australia is All About Equality

Australia has a rich history of pioneering the fight for gender equality and democratic rights. One of the most significant milestones in this regard was the implementation of universal suffrage in 1902, making Australia one of the first countries in the world to grant women the right to vote and stand for election in federal elections. This move paved the way for other nations to follow suit. It helped shape Australia's reputation as a nation that values equal representation and fair democratic processes. Today, Australia continues to strive for gender equality, with women occupying prominent positions in politics, business, and other fields.

94. Australia's Record-Breaking Cold Spells

Tucked away among the snow-capped peaks of the Australian Alps, the Charlotte Pass Ski Resort in New South Wales holds a chilly record in Australia's weather history. On June 29, 1994, temperatures plummeted to -9.4°F (-23°C), the lowest ever officially recorded in the country. This extreme cold snap underlines the contrasts in Australia's climate, from scorching deserts to icy mountain ranges. This remarkable event not only highlights the natural beauty and extremes of the Australian landscape but also marks a significant moment in the nation's meteorological history.

95. Australia's Record-Breaking Hot Spells

On January 7, 2013, the town of Oodnadatta in South Australia experienced Australia's highest-ever official temperature of 123.3°F (50.7°C). This extreme weather event highlights the harsh conditions of the Australian Outback and emphasizes the country's vulnerability to severe heatwaves. As global weather patterns continue to shift due to climate change, this record-setting temperature serves as a stark reminder of the growing challenges of extreme heat and underlines the need for urgent action to tackle climate change and promote environmental sustainability.

96. Leading Gender Equality in Soccer

Australia has made significant strides in promoting gender equality in soccer, led by Football Federation Australia's landmark decision in 2019 to ensure equal pay and shared commercial revenues for the women's Matildas and the men's Socceroos. This improved condition for the Matildas was acknowledged globally through their growing popularity. Known for their dynamic play and resilience, the Matildas have captivated audiences, with each game attracting more fans and consistently drawing sell-out crowds.

97. Australia's Bioluminescent Beaches

Imagine stepping onto a beach under the cloak of night, only to find the waves dancing with luminous blue light as if the stars have descended to play in the surf. This is no fantasy; it's a dazzling reality on Tasmania's shores in Australia, where bioluminescent beaches turn the night ocean into a canvas of glowing wonders. The architects of this spectacle are Noctiluca scintillans, tiny plankton that emit a fairy-tale glow when agitated, creating an ethereal experience for those lucky enough to witness it. It's like walking through a scene conjured by magic, a testament to the extraordinary surprises of nature.

98. Numbat or Wombat?

Australia is home to a unique marsupial called the numbat, standing out from other marsupials by being active during the day and feeding exclusively on termites. It consumes up to 20,000 of these insects every day. The numbat has evolved a long, sticky tongue to extract termites from their nests, a remarkable adaptation. Though once widespread across southern Australia, the numbat now faces the threat of extinction, and conservation efforts are in place to protect its remaining population in the wild. The numbat's existence highlights the diversity and specialized evolution of Australian marsupials, a treasure in the ecological heritage.

99. Australia and Their Lost PM

Prime Minister Harold Holt, in 1967, took a dip in the ocean at Cheviot Beach near Melbourne and became the country's most famous missing person. Despite a massive search and the sea's thorough combing, Holt was nowhere to be found - no clues, nobody, nothing. This bewildering event sparked a whirlwind of conspiracy theories, from alien abductions to secret spy missions. Holt's vanishing act remains one of the greatest mysteries down under, and people will still wonder how Australia's Prime Minister made a splash and disappeared.

100. Poo in All Shapes and Sizes

These cuddly, burrowing marsupials have baffled scientists with their ability to produce cube-shaped poop! This geometric marvel doesn't just happen by chance; it's a clever adaptation to prevent their droppings from rolling away, ensuring their scent marks stay right where they're intended. The secret behind their square scat? A unique digestive process and remarkably elastic intestines shape the feces into perfect little cubes. So, suppose you are ever wandering the Australian bush and stumble upon a collection of tiny, six-sided blocks. In that case, you'll know there's a wombat nearby, marking its territory in the most orderly fashion imaginable!

101. Australia: Too Cool for Volcanic School

Dive into Australia's sizzling secret: It's the chill-out zone of the world's continents, with no active volcano in sight! While its Pacific neighbors are rocking and rolling with volcanic fireworks, Australia's just lounging, cool as a cucumber. It's like the land down under is on a volcanic vacation, having not thrown a lava tantrum for over 4,000 years since Mount Gambier's last outburst. With its ancient volcanic vibes, this laid-back landscape makes Australia the geological oddball, where the earth prefers a silent simmer to a full-blown eruption. So, in the land of kangaroos and koalas, even the volcanoes are too relaxed to rumble!

Trivia

1. What is the name of the world's most extensive coral reef system, located off the coast of Queensland, Australia?

A) The Great Barrier Reef

B) The Red Sea Reef

C) The Amazon Reef

D) The Coral Triangle

2. Which Australian city is known for its iconic Opera House and Harbour Bridge? This city is also the capital of New South Wales.

A) Melbourne

B) Sydney

C) Brisbane

D) Perth

3. What is the official name of the vast region that covers the inside of Australia? It's known for its sand and sparse vegetation.

A) The Outback

B) The Red Desert

C) The Great Sandy Desert

D) The Bush

4. Who was Australia's first female Prime Minister, serving from 2010 to 2013?

A) Julia Gillard

B) Margaret Thatcher

C) Jacinda Ardern

D) Theresa May

5. What is the largest island off the coast of Australia, known for its rugged wilderness and wildlife?

A) Fraser Island

B) Tasmania

C) Kangaroo Island

D) New Guinea

6. In which year did Australia become a federation of colonies, formally establishing the Commonwealth of Australia?

A) 1788

B) 1901

C) 1945

D) 2000

7. What unique Australian mammal lays eggs and has a duckbill and webbed feet?

A) Kangaroo

B) Koala

C) Platypus

D) Emu

8. What is the name of the Australian national rugby team, known for its distinct gold and green colors?

A) The All Blacks

B) The Wallabies

C) The Springboks

D) The Lions

9. In 1956, which Australian city was the first to host the Summer Olympic Games?

A) Sydney

B) Melbourne

C) Brisbane

D) Perth

10. What is the indigenous name of the famous Australian rock formation?

A) Uluru

B) Mount Kosciuszko

C) Ayers Rock

D) The Olgas

11. What is the term for a rural Australian station or a large farm, especially for livestock grazing?

A) Homestead

B) Ranch

C) Outpost

D) Station

12. Which Australian town is known as the world's opal capital, where much of the mining is done underground due to high surface temperatures?

A) Coober Pedy

B) Broome

C) Kalgoorlie

D) Alice Springs

13. The "Stolen Generations" refers to the children of which group of people in Australia were forcibly removed from their families by Australian government agencies.

A) Indigenous Australians

B) Immigrants from Europe

C) Asian Australians

D) African Australians

14. Where can you find the Shrine of Remembrance, a war memorial built to honor those in World War I?

A) Melbourne

B) Canberra

C) Sydney

D) Brisbane

15. What is the unique Australian term for a dry, remote, rural area, often used to describe the vast, arid interior of the country?

A) The Outback

B) The Backcountry

C) The Bush

D) The Never-Never

16. Which Australian television personality, tragically died in 2006 after being pierced in the chest by a stingray barb?

A) David Attenborough

B) Steve Irwin

C) Bear Grylls

D) Jack Hanna

17. What is the name of the legal doctrine in Australia that deemed land uninhabited if not used in a way that European settlers deemed traditional until 1992?

A) Terra nullius

B) Jus soli

C) Aboriginal title

D) Crown land

18. Who discovered Helicobacter pylori, the bacterium responsible for most peptic ulcers?

A) Elizabeth Blackburn

B) Barry Marshall

C) Robin Warren

D) Brian Schmidt

19. The Australian coat of arms features a kangaroo and what other animal, both of which are endemic to the continent?

A) Koala

B) Emu

C) Wombat

D) Platypus

20. What is the title given to the head of government in each Australian state, equivalent to the Prime Minister at the federal level?

A) Governor

B) Premier

C) Chief Minister

D) Chancellor

21. The Yarra Valley, a renowned wine region in Australia, is located in which Australian state?

A) New South Wales

B) South Australia

C) Victoria

D) Tasmania

22. What rare geological phenomenon in Western Australia consists of living marine stromatolites believed to be one of the earliest forms of life on Earth?

A) The Pinnacles

B) Shark Bay

C) The Bungle Bungles

D) Lake Hillier

23. Which Australian won the Nobel Prize in Physiology or Medicine in 2005 for their work on the bacterium Helicobacter pylori?

A) Elizabeth Blackburn

B) Barry Marshall

C) Peter C. Doherty

D) Brian Schmidt

24. The "Ghan" is a famous train journey in Australia. What two cities are the terminus points for this route?

A) Sydney and Perth

B) Darwin and Adelaide

C) Melbourne and Brisbane

D) Canberra and Alice Springs

25. What name is given to the century gold rush era bandits known for their bush-ranging activities in Australian history?

A) Drovers

B) Convicts

C) Bushrangers

D) Swagmen

26. What is the name of the Australian Aboriginal wind instrument that is believed to be one of the world's oldest musical instruments?

A) Didgeridoo

B) Bullroarer

C) Djembe

D) Ukelele

27. Which Australian island, located south of Tasmania, is known for its rugged terrain and endemic wildlife species?

A) Lord Howe Island

B) Norfolk Island

C) Macquarie Island

D) Christmas Island

28. What was the original purpose of the Sydney Harbour Bridge when it opened in 1932?

A) Military defense

B) Pedestrian crossing

C) Railway transport

D) All of the above

29. Who was the first Australian to win the Formula One World Drivers' Championship?

A) Jack Brabham

B) Alan Jones

C) Mark Webber

D) Daniel Ricciardo

30. "Mateship" is often used in Australia to describe a cultural attitude of friendship and equality. Which event is associated with the origin of this term?

A) The Gold Rush

B) The founding of Sydney

C) World War I

D) The Federation of Australia

31. What's the title of the famous Australian painting by Frederick McCubbin depicting a person finding gold?

A) The Pioneer

B) Down on His Luck

C) Shearing the Rams

D) Across the Black Soil Plains

32. Which indigenous Australian language is known for its extensive use of click sounds, often cited as one of the most complex languages in the world?

A) Yolngu Matha

B) Warlpiri

C) Tiwi

D) Damin

33. In Australian legal history, who was the last person to be executed under the federal legal system, and in what year did this occur?

A) Ronald Ryan, 1967

B) Edward Kelly, 1880

C) Andrew Stuart, 1976

D) James Smith, 1954

34. The Great Emu War was a unique event in Australia. What was it about?

A) A conflict between emu farmers and the government

B) A military operation against emus causing agricultural damage

C) A political dispute symbolized by emus

D) A sports event named after emus

35. What is the name of the Australian philosopher best known for his work in bioethics and animal rights?

A) John Passmore

B) Peter Singer

C) David Malet Armstrong

D) Michael Tooley

36. The phenomenon known as "Morning Glory," rare rolling clouds, can be observed in which Australian region?

A) The Kimberley

B) The Gulf of Carpentaria

C) The Great Dividing Range

D) The Nullarbor Plain

37. What is the name of the Australian who won the Nobel Prize in Literature in 1973?

A) Patrick White

B) Tim Winton

C) Peter Carey

D) Richard Flanagan

38. The "Black War" refers to a period of intense conflict between British colonists and which group of indigenous Australians?

A) The Yolngu people

B) The Noongar people

C) The Tasmanian Aborigines

D) The Koori people

39. Who was the Australian Army nurse who became famous for her service during World War II and was later executed by a Japanese firing squad?

A) Nancy Wake

B) Vivian Bullwinkel

C) Florence Nightingale

D) Elizabeth Kenny

40. In Australian flora, what is the name of the unique tree known for its ability to live for more than 10,000 years?

A) Wollemi Pine

B) Huon Pine

C) King's Holly

D) Eucalyptus regnans

41. Which Australian inventor created the black box flight recorder?

A) David Warren

B) Howard Florey

C) John O'Sullivan

D) Frank Fenner

42. What significant environmental event affecting a large part of Australia is known as the "Millennium Drought"?

A) A drought that lasted from the late 1990s until 2010

B) A flood that occurred in the year 2000

C) A cyclone in the early 21st century

D) A heatwave in 1999

43. In which field did the Australian scientist Elizabeth Blackburn win a Nobel Prize for her work?

A) Physics

B) Chemistry

C) Medicine

D) Peace

44. What is the name of the Australian Aboriginal creation story, often called "The Dreaming"?

A) Tjukurpa

B) Wandjina

C) Alcheringa

D) Songlines

45. Who was the first Aboriginal Australian to serve in the Australian Parliament?

A) Neville Bonner

B) Ken Wyatt

C) Linda Burney

D) Adam Goodes

46. What is the term for the Australian underground homes built to escape the extreme heat in some parts of the country?

A) Dugouts

B) Quarters

C) Burrows

D) Earth-shelters

47. The historic shipwreck of the Batavia, a tale of mutiny and survival, occurred off the coast of which Australian region?

A) Tasmania

B) Western Australia

C) Northern Territory

D) Queensland

48. Which Australian city is known as the "Eucalyptus Capital of the World" due to its significant number of eucalyptus distilleries?

A) Bendigo

B) Wagga Wagga

C) Tamworth

D) Ingham

49. Which Australian location can the phenomenon of "Staircase to the Moon" be observed?

A) Broome

B) Darwin

C) Cairns

D) Perth

50. In Australian folklore, what is the name given to a mythical creature said to inhabit the Australian Outback, often described as a big cat?

A) Yowie

B) Bunyip

C) Drop bear

D) Phantom panther

Trivia Answers

1. A) The Great Barrier Reef

2. B) Sydney

3. A) The Outback

4. A) Julia Gillard

5. B) Tasmania

6. B) 1901

7. C) Platypus

8. B) The Wallabies

9. B) Melbourne

10. A) Ularu

11. D) Station

12. A) Coober Pedy

13. A) Indigenous Australians

14. A) Melbourne

15. D) The Never-Never

16. B) Steve Irwin

17. A) Terra nullius

18. B) Barry Marshall

19. B) Emu

20. B) Premier

21. C) Victoria

22. B) Shark Bay

23. B) Barry Marshall

24. B) Darwin and Adelaide

25. C) Bushrangers

26. A) Didgeridoo

27. C) Macquarie Island

28. D) All of the above

29. A) Jack Brabham

30. C) World War I

31. B) Down on His Luck

32. D) Damin

33. A) Ronald Ryan, 1967

34. B) A military operation against emus causing agricultural damage

35. B) Peter Singer

36. B) The Gulf of Carpentaria

37. A) Patrick White

38. C) The Tasmanian Aborigines

39. B) Vivian Bullwinkel

40. C) King's Holly

41. A) David Warren

42. A) A drought that lasted from the late 1990s until 2010

43. C) Medicine

44. C) Alcheringa

45. A) Neville Bonner

46. A) Dugouts

47. B) Western Australia

48. B) Wagga Wagga

49. A) Broome

50. D) Phantom panther

How'd You Score?

Person 1: Score _____   **/ 50**

Person 2: Score _____   **/ 50**

Person 3: Score _____   **/ 50**

Person 4: Score _____   **/ 50**

Person 5: Score _____   **/ 50**

19-25: Aussie Explorer

You are embarking on a thrilling journey through Australia's vast landscapes and rich history. As an Aussie Explorer, you buzz with excitement and curiosity. You've scratched the surface of Australia's wonders – now it's time to delve deeper into its cultural heritage and natural beauty. Keep your spirit of adventure alive, and soon you'll be navigating the Outback like a pro!

26-32: Rising Star Down Under

Not bad at all! You're exploring the depths of Australia's unique environment and culture with the enthusiasm of a budding adventurer. Your knowledge is blooming like the wildflowers of the Kimberley, but there's still so much more to uncover. Stay passionate, and you'll soon be decoding Aussie trivia like a seasoned bushwalker!

33-39: Australian Aficionado

Impressive, very impressive! You're advancing in your journey Down Under, showcasing an understanding that even a local would admire. Like an aficionado learning the secrets of the Australian bush, you're navigating through the country's history and landscapes with promising skill.

Keep honing your knowledge, and you might just become an Australian trivia expert!

40-46: Outback Oracle

Congratulations, you're a powerhouse of knowledge when it comes to Australia! With a mental archive as vast as the Australian continent, you're navigating through its intricate tales and natural wonders with the confidence of a true Outback Oracle. Keep this spectacular momentum, and you might just become a legend in Australian trivia!

47-50: Australian Trivia Royalty

Spectacular! You've reached a level of expertise that would make even the most knowledgeable Aussie historians proud. With insight as deep as the Great Barrier Reef and a memory as impressive as the Sydney Opera House, you're not just a fan of Australia – you're the reigning monarch of Australian trivia!

Thank You

Dear reader,

I want to express my deepest gratitude to you for embarking on this journey with me through "Facts of Australia - Interesting Stories and Trivia about the Land Down Under." Your interest and support have made this experience truly special.

While putting together this book, I've learned so many fascinating things, enjoyed countless cups of tea, and had a lot of support from my family. Each fact in this book is a testament to how much we want to explore Australia's mysteries and challenge what we thought we knew.

This book has been a labor of love, driven by my desire to unite people in their admiration for Australia. The stories and moments shared in these pages are all about passion, laughter, and a fascination with the unique things that make Australia.

Your feedback is critical to me, and I can't wait to hear your thoughts and feelings about the book. Whether you loved it, had some constructive criticism, or wanted to share how much it meant to you, your feedback inspires and motivates us.

Your review means a lot. You can leave your feedback on Amazon by scanning the QR code.

Thank you for being an integral part of this journey. Your presence and interest have made it all the more meaningful.

With heartfelt thanks and warmest wishes,

Ella Wallaby

Made in the USA
Las Vegas, NV
10 November 2024

11495542R00079